FREAKY
SCIENCE
DISCOVERIES

BY SARAH MACHAJEWSKI

Gareth Stevens
PUBLISHING

Please visit our website, www.garethstevens.com. For a free color catalog of all our high-quality books, call toll free 1-800-542-2595 or fax 1-877-542-2596.

Library of Congress Cataloging-in-Publication Data

Machajewski, Sarah, author.
Freaky science discoveries / Sarah Machajewski.
    pages cm. — (Freaky true science)
Includes bibliographical references and index.
ISBN 978-1-4824-2952-7 (pbk.)
ISBN 978-1-4824-2953-4 (6 pack)
ISBN 978-1-4824-2954-1 (library binding)
1. Science—History—Juvenile literature. 2. Discoveries in science—Juvenile literature. I. Title.
Q126.4.M315 2016
509—dc23
                                    2015000349

First Edition

Published in 2016 by
Gareth Stevens Publishing
111 East 14th Street, Suite 349
New York, NY 10003

Designer: Sarah Liddell
Editor: Ryan Nagelhout

Photo credits: Cover, backgroud throughout book andrey_l/Shutterstock.com; Cover, pp. 1 (microscope and cylinder used througout book) Morphart Creation/Shutterstock.com; cover, p. 1 (bacteria) goa novi/Shutterstock.com; cover, p. 5 George Hales/Hulton Archive/Getty Images; pp. 5, 7, 9, 11, 13, 15, 17, 19, 21, 23, 25, 27, 29 (hand used throughout) Helena Ohman/Shutterstock.com; pp. 5, 7, 9, 11, 13, 15, 17, 19, 21, 23, 25, 27, 29 (texture throughout) Alex Gontar/Shutterstock.com; p. 6 photo courtesy of NASA/Alan Bean; p. 7 Hulton Archive/Stringer/Getty Images; p. 9 (main) Universal History Archive/Getty Images; p. 9 (prism) Ian Cuming/Ikon Images/Getty Images; p. 11 (main) Alfred Eisenstaedt/Contributor/The LIFE Picture Collection/Getty Images; p. 11 (petri dish) Guntars Grebezs/E+/Getty Images; p. 13 (main) Dr. Fred Hossler/Visuals Unlimited/Getty Images; p. 13 (petri dish) BIOPHOTO ASSOCIATES/Science Source/Getty Images; p. 15 (main) DEA/S. VANNINI/Contributor/De Agostini/Getty Images; p. 15 (inset) Edward Kinsman/Science Source/Getty Images; p. 17 Print Collector/Contributor/Hulton Archive/Getty Images; p. 19 SCIENCE SOURCE/Science Source/Getty Images; p. 19 (inset) Ranveig/Wikimedia Commons; p. 21 crochet.david/Wikimedia Commons; p. 23 LAGUNA DESIGN/Science Photo Library/Getty Images; p. 24 xpixel/Shutterstock.com; p. 25 SCOTT CAMAZINE/Science Source/Getty Images; p. 27 (graphic) Encyclopaedia Britannica/UIG/Getty Images; p. 27 (Dolly) Getty Images/Handout/Getty Images News/Getty Images; p. 29 Sean Murphy/Stone/Getty Images.

Printed in the United States of America

CPSIA compliance information: Batch #CS15GS: For further information contact Gareth Stevens, New York, New York at 1-800-542-2595.

CONTENTS

Words in the glossary appear in **bold** type
the first time they are used in the text.

SCIENCE RULES!

Science rules our world. It shows up in all parts of our life, from the tiniest single-celled organisms to the enormous planets in our solar system. Think about it: science plays a part in almost everything. The way your nerves carry messages from your brain to parts of your body—that's science. What about the way batteries power all sorts of electronic devices? That's science, too!

Science makes our world and the things in it work. But sometimes science surprises us. When these surprises pop up, things can get a little freaky. These freaky occurrences can have a great effect on how we understand things and sometimes change our thinking forever. Let's explore some of the freakiest science discoveries that have surprised us, shocked us, and changed our world.

FREAKY FACTS!

Discovering something freaky begins with someone noticing something weird and asking "why." This skill, called observation, has uncovered information that has changed our world forever.

WHAT IS SCIENCE?

The word "science" may create several different pictures in your head. You may think of test tubes and chemical reactions, or you may think of someone observing the stars through a telescope. You may even picture an exploding volcano! "Science" is a small word that covers big territory. In this book, we'll examine freaky discoveries that have happened in all different fields of science, including medicine, biology, animal science, space science, and more.

MORE OF SCIENCE'S SURPRISING SECRETS ARE JUST WAITING TO BE DISCOVERED.

WHAT FALLS FASTER?

Gravity affects us every day, but we can't feel it. Gravity is the force that pulls objects, including us, toward Earth's center. Before the 16th century, scientists couldn't explain why things moved the way they did.

Our general belief was that heavy objects fall faster than light objects. Since heavy objects have more **mass**, they should drop more quickly, right? Wrong! According to legend, a scientist named Galileo Galilei did experiments in the 1500s that proved this to be false. Stories say that he dropped a heavy object and a light object off the Leaning Tower of Pisa at the same time. The objects fell at the same speed! This went against everything people had believed to be true.

FREAKY FACTS!

Astronauts later re-created this experiment on the moon. Apollo 15 astronaut David Scott dropped a falcon feather and hammer at the same time, and they fell at the same speed!

NOBODY KNOWS FOR SURE IF GALILEO ACTUALLY DROPPED OBJECTS OFF THE LEANING TOWER OF PISA. WHETHER IT HAPPENED OR NOT, GALILEO'S SCIENCE PROVED THAT OBJECTS OF DIFFERENT WEIGHTS FALL AT THE SAME SPEED.

THE HAILSTORM

Galileo said his idea for this experiment came to him during a hailstorm. He noticed small hailstones and big hailstones hit the ground at the same time. Galileo lived during a time when new or weird scientific ideas were often rejected. You could even be punished for ideas that didn't follow religious teachings. People in the 16th century didn't believe many of Galileo's ideas, but today we know why Galileo's freaky experiment works.

NEWTON'S
GREAT DISCOVERIES

Isaac Newton was a scientist whose discoveries changed the world forever. Using math and physics, he explained how gravity works. He also came up with three laws that explained how objects move when force is applied to them.

Newton experimented with color and light, too. In 1665, he shut himself in a darkened room. He cut a hole in his window that allowed one beam of light to shine through. Newton then placed a glass **prism** in front of the light. It split into a rainbow of colors! Then, he placed a second prism upside down in front of the colored light. It turned back into white light. Newton was the first to discover that white light is made of all the colors we can see.

FREAKY FACTS!

Newton greatly influenced Albert Einstein. In the early 1900s, Einstein built upon Newton's theories about gravity to come up with his own revolutionary ideas about light and gravity.

PRISM

NEWTON DISCOVERED WHAT'S CALLED THE COLOR SPECTRUM. HE WAS THE FIRST PERSON TO USE THE WORD "SPECTRUM" TO DESCRIBE THE RANGE OF COLORS THAT MAKES UP WHITE LIGHT.

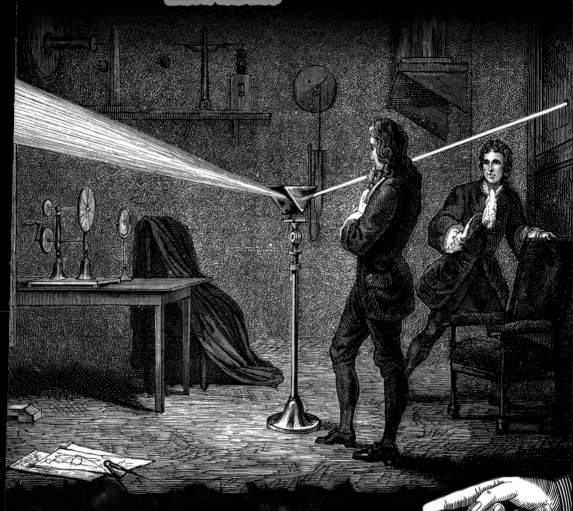

SUN AT THE CENTER

While Newton was alive, many people thought Earth was the center of the solar system. Some scientists thought the sun was at the center, but couldn't prove it. Newton's experiments and math calculations confirmed that Earth and the other planets orbit the sun because of the way gravity acts on them. His scientific discoveries proved once and for all that the sun was the center of our solar system.

ACCIDENTAL ANTIBIOTICS

Antibiotics are considered one of the most important scientific discoveries of all time. They're a kind of medicine that helps us fight **infections**. However, antibiotics have only been around for less than 100 years—and their discovery was a complete accident!

In 1928, a Scottish scientist named Alexander Fleming was studying bacteria that made people sick. He had placed samples of bacteria in dishes, but put them aside when he left on vacation. When he returned, he found his samples **contaminated** with mold! He thought his experiments were ruined. As Fleming went to throw away his samples, he noticed something very freaky. The bacteria had spread all over the petri dish it was being grown in, except for an area with a big, moldy blob. The area around the mold was bacteria-free!

FREAKY FACTS!

The ancient Egyptians used mold to fight infections long before Fleming's discovery. They put pieces of moldy bread on infected wounds to help them heal.

PENICILLIN

GOOD MISTAKES

Before his freaky lab discovery, Alexander Fleming had a feeling
that there had to be something that could help fight bacteria.
In 1921, he discovered lysozyme, a chemical found in tears and oth
bodily fluids. This was an accidental discovery, too! Some fluid ha
leaked from his nose as he bent over a sample of bacteria. It hur
the bacteria a little bit, but wasn't strong enough. It took 7 mor

Fleming was surprised by his moldy accident. It was as if something in the mold killed the bacteria or kept it from spreading. This seemed odd, but promising—maybe this mold could kill bacterial infections inside people's bodies. Fleming took samples of the mold and ran some tests. The mold was from the *Penicillium notatum* group. It would later be used to make a medicine called penicillin.

Penicillin changed the world forever. Though it was discovered in 1928, it wasn't widely produced or used as medicine until the 1940s. Pencillin is an important medicine because it kills bacteria that causes sore throats, a dangerous disease called meningitis, and more. Millions of lives have been saved thanks to Fleming and his accidental, yet fortunate, discovery.

FREAKY FACTS!

The first person to be treated with penicillin was a policeman named Albert Alexander. A simple scratch had turned into a life-threatening infection of his eyes, face, and lungs. Penicillin helped him recover, but only temporarily—he died a few days later, because they didn't have enough to treat him properly.

OFF THE WALL

Penicillin works because it hits bacteria where it hurts: their cell wall. Cell walls protect bacteria from harm. If bacteria aren't harmed, they can keep growing. When the penicillin mold came into contact with the bacteria in Fleming's petri dish, it weakened the bacteria's cell walls, causing them to break. However, some bacteria have learned how to fight back. They produce substances that kill the mold's ability to destroy their cell wall! Freaky!

PENICILLIUM NOTATUM SPORES

ON THE CELLULAR LEVEL, EVERYTHING IS A FIGHT FOR SURVIVAL. PENICILLIN ACTED LIKE A WONDER DRUG FOR A WHILE, BUT THEN SOME BACTERIA FOUGHT BACK. THEY PRODUCED NEW **STRAINS** OF BACTERIA THAT WERE RESISTANT TO PENICILLIN, MAKING THE MEDICINE INEFFECTIVE.

PENICILLIN

RESISTANT BACTERIUM

13

FUNKY, FREAKY CHEESE

Mold and bacteria are pretty freaky, but what's even freakier is that they can make some foods taste really good. The thought of eating mold or bacteria might seem weird, but you've probably eaten them before. They help make some of the best-tasting cheeses!

The art of making cheese is a matter of science. When an **enzyme** called rennet comes into contact with milk, it separates the milk into curds, which are solid, and whey, a liquid. The real science begins next, when cheese is left to ripen and age.

Cheese makers purposely add bacteria and mold to their cheese. The bacteria and mold feed on the cheese's sugars, changing the flavor and texture. Flavorless curds can start tasting like butter, and odorless cheese can start to smell sweet. Have you ever tried blue cheese? Its funky smell and dark, blue-green lines are made by mold.

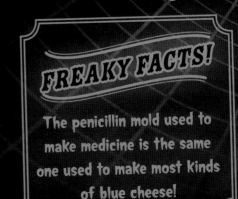

FREAKY FACTS!

The penicillin mold used to make medicine is the same one used to make most kinds of blue cheese!

CHEESE, PLEASE!

The first cheese was probably made by accident. Legend has it that 4,000 years ago, a man put milk in a bag made from a sheep's stomach. He left it there for several hours, not thinking anything special would happen. Inside, the stomach contained rennet, which reacted with the milk. The chemical reaction separated the milk into curds and whey. When the man opened his bag, he found a very delicious treat!

ROENTGEN'S RAYS

For years, the only way we could see inside the human body was to cut someone open. In 1895, a scientist discovered a way to look inside using **electromagnetic** energy.

Wilhelm Roentgen began studying electrical rays in the late 1800s. He tested how electric current passed through gas inside a glass tube. During one experiment, he darkened the room, turned on the current, and noticed something odd: a piece of cardboard nearby that had been painted with **fluorescent** material was glowing!

The cardboard was glowing because it had absorbed a kind of ray that hadn't been discovered yet: X-rays. Later, Roentgen learned many objects could absorb this kind of energy—including bones. For the first time, it was possible to see inside the body without going under the knife!

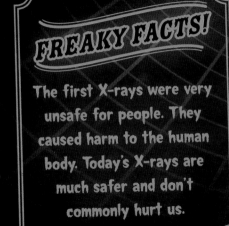

FREAKY FACTS!

The first X-rays were very unsafe for people. They caused harm to the human body. Today's X-rays are much safer and don't commonly hurt us.

BONY HANDS

At first, Roentgen experimented with the newly discovered rays by putting his hand between the light source and a screen. He could see his hand projected on the screen behind it, but he wanted something more permanent. He replaced the screen with a photographic plate, making it possible to take pictures. The first official X-ray was of his wife's hand. In it, you can see the bones of her fingers and her wedding ring!

CURIE AND RADIATION

About a year after Roentgen discovered X-rays, French scientist Henri Becquerel discovered another kind of ray, quite by surprise! He had been experimenting with minerals to see if there was a connection between materials that give off light and X-rays. In 1896, Becquerel put a mineral that contained the element uranium and a photographic plate in a drawer. A few days later, he developed the plate and found the **silhouette** of the samples! What caused this to happen?

Shortly after, scientist Marie Curie gave it a name: **radioactivity**. She theorized that an object was radioactive if it was made of radioactive elements, such as uranium. However, experiments showed her that some objects were more radioactive than uranium. This led to the discovery of two new radioactive elements, radium and polonium.

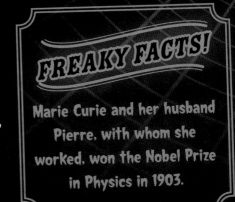

FREAKY FACTS!

Marie Curie and her husband Pierre, with whom she worked, won the Nobel Prize in Physics in 1903.

POLISH SCIENTIST MARIE CURIE WAS THE FIRST FEMALE PROFESSOR AT THE UNIVERSITY OF PARIS.

URANIUM RADIATION

SILHOUETTE

DANGEROUS RAYS

Marie Curie made incredible advances in science thanks to her close work with radioactive materials. However, no one at the time knew how dangerous her work was. When radiation enters the body, it destroys cells, alters their genetic material, and causes cancer. Marie Curie kept test tubes of radioactive materials in her home and even carried them in her pocket! She was sick all the time and died in 1934 of a blood disease caused by exposure to radiation.

BLACK HOLES

Sometimes gravity does weird things. What if an object's gravitational pull was so strong that nothing could escape it—not even light? That's a black hole.

A black hole is a really strange space oddity. It's a region of space where matter has collapsed inward because of the pull of gravity. You can't see or touch them, but black holes are there. Black holes swallow up the light from nearby stars. Any object that comes near a black hole gets sucked in, too! If a person were to fall into a black hole, their body would be ripped apart by the extreme force of gravity. That's freaky!

Black holes can't be "discovered" because we can't see them. However, the first evidence of a black hole was discovered in 1971. There's still much to learn about these weird space objects.

FREAKY FACTS!

Cygnus X-1 is about 6,070 light-years from Earth and spins around more than 800 times a second! Freaky!

THE X-RAY STAR

In 1971, scientists found evidence of the first space matter to be officially considered a black hole. They noticed a star, Cygnus X-1, was oddly affected by something nearby that no one could see. Cygnus X-1 appeared to be giving off X-rays, but it wasn't the kind of star that could do that alone. Something else had to have been causing this. Scientists determined it was an undetectable mass—the first official black hole.

THERE ARE MANY FORCES IN SPACE WE CAN'T SEE. WE KNOW THEY EXIST ONLY BECAUSE WE SEE THE EFFECT THEY HAVE ON PLANETS AND STARS.

IS TIME TRAVEL POSSIBLE?

Sometimes the freakiest scientific discoveries exist only on paper. But that doesn't mean they aren't real. In 1935, scientists Albert Einstein and Nathan Rosen theorized that time travel was possible. It could happen with wormholes.

Einstein and Rosen theorized that space and time are a **continuous** thing. However, using math, they determined certain parts of space-time could fold over on itself. They then said a tube could form between the sides of the fold and connect two parts of space-time that would normally be very far away from each other. Called a wormhole, this would be a shortcut between two points in the same universe or even different universes! This shortcut would be a way for people or objects to jump ahead in time, traveling faster than the speed of light.

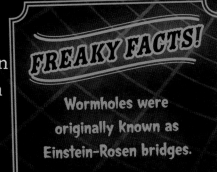

FREAKY FACTS!

Wormholes were originally known as Einstein-Rosen bridges.

SEARCHING FOR WORMHOLES

Wormholes are truly freaky, but we have yet to discover one. So far, time travel has only existed in science fiction. Scientists believe that if a wormhole were found, it would actually be impossible to travel through. Most think wormholes would collapse instantly. However, scientists also think the presence of something called "exotic" matter could hold a wormhole open and keep it from collapsing. But, like wormholes, no one knows if exotic matter actually exists!

MAGIC MAGGOTS

Maggots are pretty freaky insects. They creep, they crawl, and they ooze slime. The last place you'd want them is inside your body, right? Think again! When maggots are placed inside a cut, they get to work doing what they do best: chowing down on rotting flesh.

It can take a long time for big cuts to heal. Wounds can become infected and make someone really sick. Maggots are helpful because they eat up all the dead tissue. This clears the way for healthy tissue to grow back. Scientists think that maggot slime plays a big role in the healing process, too. If a person's body makes too much of a protein that helps heal wounds, the presence of maggot slime tells the body to back off. Yuck!

FREAKY FACTS!

The US Food and Drug Administration approved maggot therapy in 2004.

ANCIENT MEDICINE

People have been putting maggots into their own bodies for centuries. It might seem strange that people actually want to put flesh-eating bugs inside and on their bodies. After all, maggots are mostly found on garbage and rotting corpses. However, maggots have no appetite for living tissue: They just want the dead stuff! And maggot therapy seems to work—one scientific study claims maggots can help heal anywhere from 50 to 80 percent of common wounds.

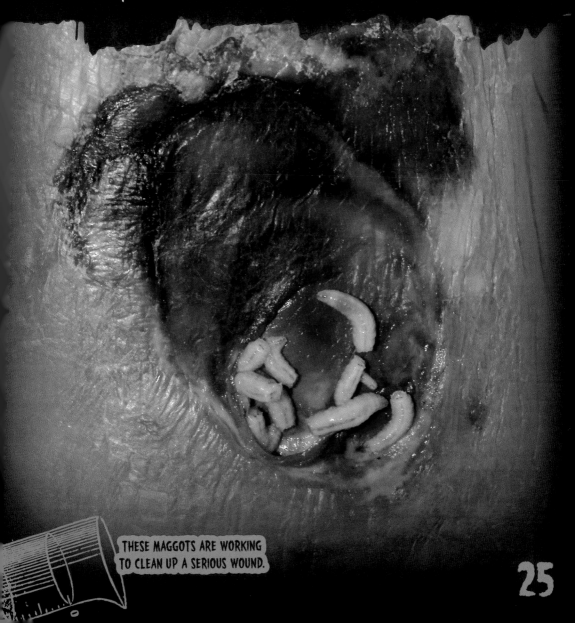

THESE MAGGOTS ARE WORKING TO CLEAN UP A SERIOUS WOUND.

DOUBLE TROUBLE

Have you ever thought what it would be like to make an exact copy of yourself? Single-celled organisms have been doing this for millions of years. Cloning is the process of making an exact copy of a living thing. The original and its clone are identical, or exactly the same. They share the same **DNA**.

This process rarely happens naturally in humans because there are a countless number of genetic combinations an organism can get from its parents. However, in the late 1990s, scientists in Scotland discovered how to control this process. Dolly the sheep was born on July 5, 1996. Her DNA was identical to the DNA scientists took from another sheep to make her. Though she only lived for 6 years, Dolly was a major breakthrough in the science of cloning.

FREAKY FACTS!

Dolly was the only clone that survived out of 277 attempts made during the experiments in Scotland.

CLONING DOLLY

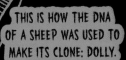

THIS IS HOW THE DNA OF A SHEEP WAS USED TO MAKE ITS CLONE: DOLLY.

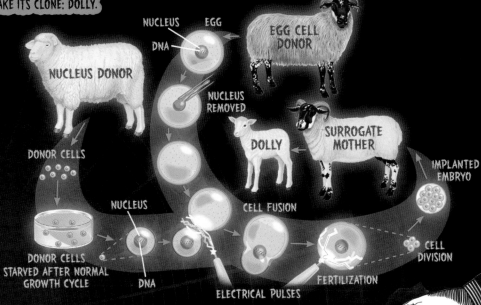

NUCLEUS DONOR

NUCLEUS   EGG

DNA

EGG CELL DONOR

NUCLEUS REMOVED

DONOR CELLS

DOLLY

SURROGATE MOTHER

NUCLEUS

IMPLANTED EMBRYO

CELL FUSION

DONOR CELLS STARVED AFTER NORMAL GROWTH CYCLE

DNA

ELECTRICAL PULSES

FERTILIZATION

CELL DIVISION

SHOULD WE DO IT?

Many people think cloning shouldn't be allowed because it can lead down a dangerous road. They worry that picking and choosing which genes to copy could have dangerous consequences for our future. However, other people think cloning could make strong, healthy animals. They think cloning could even help humans! The success of Dolly brought this debate into households all over the world. How do you feel about human cloning?

27

THE FREAKY FUTURE

For hundreds of years, scientific discovery has turned our world on its head several times over. It has changed the way we think about tiny organisms and giant space matter. It's forced us to rethink what we know about animals and ourselves. Scientific discovery has even pushed us to eat mold and fill our own bodies with maggots!

Some of the most important scientific discoveries are also some of the freakiest. However, once weird science is discovered, it proves that unbelievable things can sometimes be true. Science can be unpredictable, but if there is one thing that's certain, it's that science is constantly changing. There's no telling what the next freaky scientific development will be or who will uncover it. Could it be you?

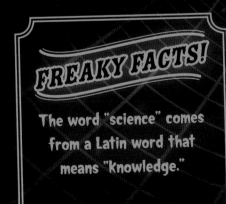

FREAKY FACTS!

The word "science" comes from a Latin word that means "knowledge."

FREAKY FICTION

Certain well-known science oddities are just plain untrue. Here are some of the most common mistaken ideas:

- Lightning never strikes the same place twice. False! There's no reason why lightning can't strike the same place again and again.

- Urinating on a jellyfish sting makes it hurt less. False! It may actually make the sting more painful!

- People can get warts by touching toads. False! Warts are caused by viruses, not amphibians.

AS WE EXPLORE MORE OF OUR WORLD, WE'VE LEARNED THAT THE FREAKIEST THINGS ARE NOT FICTION—THEY'RE FACT.

GLOSSARY

contaminate: to make something impure

continuous: unbroken

DNA: a molecule in the body that carries genetic information, which gives the instructions for life

electromagnetic: having the property of being magnetized or electrically charged

enzyme: a protein made in the body that helps chemical changes occur

fluorescent: having the ability to glow or shine

infection: the spread of germs inside the body, causing illness

mass: the amount of matter in something

prism: an object with surfaces that have the ability to separate white light into a color spectrum

radioactivity: the putting out of harmful energy in the form of tiny particles

silhouette: the outline of an object

strain: a type of organism that comes from an earlier, common ancestor

FOR MORE INFORMATION

BOOKS

Lake, Matt, and Randy Fairbanks. *Weird Science: Mad Marvels from the Way-Out World*. New York, NY: Sterling Children's Books, 2012.

Margles, Samantha. *Mythbusters Science Fair Book*. New York, NY: Scholastic, 2011.

WEBSITES

Science
kids.usa.gov/science
Kids.gov Science is a great resource for all things science related.

Science Games
discoverykids.com/category/science
Discovery Kids introduces children to the fantastic world of science with fun games.

Publisher's note to educators and parents: Our editors have carefully reviewed these websites to ensure that they are suitable for students. Many websites change frequently, however, and we cannot guarantee that a site's future contents will continue to meet our high standards of quality and educational value. Be advised that students should be closely supervised whenever they access the Internet.

INDEX